NATURE AND THE DIVINE NAMES

First published in the UK by Beacon Books and Media Ltd
Earl Business Centre, Dowry Street, Oldham, OL8 2PF, UK.
Copyright © Farrah Iftikhar 2025

www.beaconbooks.net

Cataloging-in-Publication record for this book is available from the British Library

ISBN 978-1-916955-83-7 Paperback
ISBN 978-1-916955-84-4 Hardback
ISBN 978-1-916955-85-1 Ebook

Cover design by Raees Mahmood Khan

NATURE AND THE DIVINE NAMES

Farrah Iftikhar

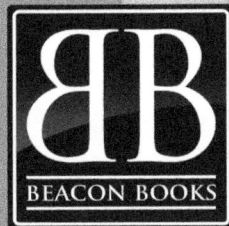

BEACON BOOKS

بسم الله الرحيم

This book is dedicated to Dawud and Ibrahim

INTRODUCTION

WHAT IS THE INTENTION OF THIS BOOK?

The first intention is to connect the reader to Allah and draw closer to Him through His Beautiful Names, by reflecting on the nature around us.

The second intention is to encourage the reader to spend more time in nature and to truly connect with it. One of the ways in which this can be done is by reflecting on the qualities of Allah.

The third intention is to gain a deeper understanding and comprehension of Allah's Names, by studying them through a lens which one is familiar with, i.e. the nature around us.

WHO IS THIS BOOK FOR?

This book is for people of all ages. I intend for this book to become one which families explore together; one which children and adults carry with them on their adventures and excursions through nature.

AR-RAHMAN
The All Merciful

الرَّحْمٰن

Allah is Ar-Rahman. Allah is the Most Kind, the Most Loving and the Most Merciful. Allah's mercy covers ALL of His creation. Nobody is left out.

Allah loves us more than anybody else in this world. Think of all the blessings He has given us which we didn't even have to ask for. Allah's love is unconditional.

Ar-Rahman is like the sun. The sun does not discriminate between people. The sun shines its light and gives warmth to everyone and everything. This quality is a reminder of Allah's love and compassion. Allah's love and mercy encompasses everyone and everything.

Have you observed animal mothers with their babies? They are very loving and affectionate towards their offspring. For example, a cow will groom her calf for hours and goat mums will sleep side by side with their babies, even wrapping their necks around each other until they are older.

AL-QUDDUS
The Absolutely Pure

القُدُّوسُ

Allah is Al-Quddus. He is the Absolutely Pure. Allah is Holy and Pure. Allah is perfect and free from any imperfections.
Allah's Name Al-Quddus shows us that it is impossible for us to imagine the greatness of Allah. There is absolutely nothing like Him.

Trees and forests purify the air that we breathe. Trees absorb toxic gases from the atmosphere, making the air purer for us. Trees release pure oxygen for us to breathe in. This is a reminder that Allah is Absolutely Pure and loves purity.

Have you ever observed the crystal clear water in a spring or at the top of a mountain? This water is so pure. Just like Allah is The Absolutely Pure. Allah likes for us to be pure before we pray salah or read the Qur'an. We can use this pure water to make ourselves pure.

AS-SALAAM
The Giver of Peace

السَّلَامُ

Allah is As-Salaam. Allah is the Giver of Peace. Salaam means peace, safety, security. In Allah we feel all of these. We feel safe and secure knowing He is always there for us, and we feel peace simply by remembering Him. Allah is the source of peace. Salaam also means to be free from imperfections, to be flawless. Allah is the only One who is completely flawless. For this reason true peace can only be found in Him.

When we take a walk in the woods, amongst the trees, in the park or any other green space, we feel a sense of peace descending on us. These green spaces help us to feel calm and balanced. We should thank As-Salaam, who is the source of peace and who has created these places to have such an effect.

Blue spaces refer to rivers, seas, canals, etc. Rather like green spaces, these bodies of water also have the power to help us feel calm. The sound of the waves crashing or the water flowing bring about tranquillity. Whenever we feel a sense of peace, we should remind ourselves of the Giver of Peace: Allah.

AL-MUHAYMIN
The Protector

Allah is Al-Muhaymin: The Protector. Allah is the One who ensures the wellbeing and protection of His creation. Allah is the Guardian. In this Name, we find peace and comfort knowing that are being well looked after, that we are in the best hands.

When a mother hen senses danger she clucks at her chicks who run under her wings and stay there until the danger has passed. In fact, one of the meanings of the root of Muhaymin is "to extend a wing" (like a hen protecting her chicks!). Allah has given this instinct of protection to all animals and humans. This quality helps creation to continue to live and thrive.

Beavers build dams across streams to make ponds where they can create safe homes called "lodges". These ponds protect them from predators like wolves, coyotes, and mountain lions. The ponds also help plants grow and provide homes for other animals, keeping the forest healthy. The way beavers protect and care for their environment reminds us of Allah's quality as The Protector.

AL-MUTAKABBIR
The Supreme

Allah is Al-Mutakabbir. Allah is Majestic and so Vast. Allah possesses all greatness and needs nobody. "Allahu Akbar" comes from the same root. Allah cannot be harmed by anyone. Another meaning of Al-Mutakabbir is The Most Proud. This does not mean that Allah is arrogant. It means He is Supreme and above everyone and everything else.

Have you ever looked at the ocean? The water seems to go on and on with no end in sight. We can't even begin to imagine how much water there is. The oceans are so vast and are home to millions of creatures. Looking at the oceans should remind of us of how vast and great Allah is.

Just like when we look at the ocean, we feel the same sense of awe when we look up at a mountain. Mountains are so huge and majestic, they make us feel tiny in comparison. They fill us with awe and wonder and remind of us of how great and supreme the Creator of these mountains must be. They remind of us of Al-Mutakabbir.

AL-KHALIQ
The Creator

الْخَالِقُ

Allah is Al-Khaliq, the Creator. Allah is the One who brings everything into existence. Allah continues to create in every moment. He creates every movement and every breath we take. Allah is the only One who determines when, how and what to create. Allah has created everything perfectly.

Look up at the sky at night. The sky looks so vast and enormous. We see the stars twinkling and the glow from the Milky Way, inspiring awe and wonder. Looking at the night sky reminds us of the artistry of Al-Khaliq, the Creator. We should feel so much reverence for our Creator.

We can see Al-Khaliq in all of creation, since Allah has created and is creating everything. This includes every single movement and action. For example, if we see a horse galloping, it is Allah who is creating movement in the horse's body which is causing it to gallop.

AL-MUSAWWIR
The Shaper

المصور

Allah is Al-Musawwir, the Shaper or the Fashioner. Allah gives everything He creates a special and unique form. Allah arranges forms and colours and is the shaper of beauty. Allah brings into existence whatever He wills and in whatever manner He wills it.

Have you ever looked at a pineapple closely? Pineapples have such a unique shape and texture. Apparently, the spikes stop predators from eating them! Next time you buy a pineapple, look at its patterns and run your hand over it to feel its texture. Remind yourself of Al-Musawwir – the Shaper, who gave the pineapple its unique shape.

Rather like pineapples, butterflies have a unique shape, one that is very appealing to the eye. There are more than 160,000 species of butterfly and each come with their own unique patterns. Try to observe the butterflies you see fluttering around you, looking at their detailed patterns and remember Al-Musawwir, the One who fashioned them.

AL-GHAFFAR
The Great Forgiver

الغفّار

Allah is Al-Ghaffar, the Great Forgiver. You may commit the same mistake over and over again but if you turn to Allah, He will forgive you. Al-Ghaffar's forgiveness is continuous and repetitive. Allah never tires of forgiving us. Sometimes we may feel like we are not worthy of His forgiveness but Allah's attribute of Al-Ghaffar shows us we should never despair and continuously turn back to Him.

Every morning the rising of the sun marks the beginning of a new day. Every sunrise is an opportunity to start afresh and reset. When Allah forgives us, it is a new beginning for us. Allah's forgiveness wipes away our sins just like the sunrise wipes away the darkness of the night. The sunrise is a reminder of Al-Ghaffar, the Great Forgiver.

Bees produce a sticky substance called propolis, which they use to seal cracks and repair their hives. Interestingly, one of the root meanings of Al-Ghaffar refers to this substance being used by Arabs to fill cracks in their leather water skins to prevent leaks. Just as propolis fixes and renews the beehives, Allah's forgiveness offers us protection and a chance for renewal.

AL-WAHHAB
The Giver of Gifts

الوَهَّاب

Allah is Al-Wahhab, the Giver of Gifts. Allah blesses us with many gifts and blessings each and every day. Al-Wahhab gives continuously without expecting anything in return. Allah's gifts to us are free and plenty.

When a cloud gets heavy with lots of water, it rains. The rain comes down continuously and freely with no breaks in the flow. This is how Allah blesses us with gifts. Allah's blessings to us are continuous and free-flowing. There are no breaks in His giving. Next time you see a grey cloud and it begins to rain, remind yourself that Allah's blessings rain down on us in a similar way.

The very existence of earth and its resources demonstrates Allah's generosity. The earth provides us with everything we need to live, such as water, food, and shelter. Whenever we look around we should try to acknowledge these gifts and acknowledge the One who gives us these gifts freely: Al-Wahhab.

AL-FATTAH
The Opener

الفَتَّاحُ

Allah is Al-Fattah, the Opener. Allah is the One who opens the gates of mercy and victory to whomever He wishes. Allah opens up solutions to problems and opportunities. When we think one door is closing, Allah is opening another door for us.

When spring arrives and we see the buds on the trees opening and eventually becoming blossom, this is a reminder of Allah's name, Al-Fattah. He is the Opener and causes everything to open. The opening of the blossom symbolises renewal and growth. Also, when we say someone has 'blossomed' we mean they have become confident or successful. We should turn to Al-Fattah if these are qualities we are seeking to achieve.

When we see a bird's wings open, preparing to fly, we are reminded of Al-Fattah, the One who causes the wings to open. Flying depicts freedom and overcoming our fears and worries. When we see a bird flying we can remind ourselves that worshipping Al-Fattah, the Opener, will lead to our freedom and Allah will open many new doors for us.

AL-BASIT
The Expander

البَاسِط

Allah is Al-Basit, the Expander. Allah is the One who widens. Al-Basit also refers to the One who increases in how much He gives; His giving is endless. Allah is the One who releases joy, comfort and abundance into us. Allah expands and widens our hearts and souls and gives us sustenance in His Generosity and Mercy.

The sea is very expansive. When we stand in front of the sea, it is vast and stretches further than the eye can see into the horizon. There seems no end to the water; there is an abundance of it. The sea is a beautiful example of firstly that Allah is the One who expands, the one who has expanded the sea and made it so vast. Secondly, the sea shows that Allah gives in abundance. There is no limit to His giving.

Deserts are very vast and expansive. They stretch out for miles and miles. Deserts manifest Allah's boundless nature; there is no end to His giving. This is one of the meanings of Al-Basit. Deserts are so hot and dry, but there is still life there: animals, plants, and even humans live in deserts. This is a reminder that Al-Basit is the One who can provide and give us blessings even in the most unlikely of places.

AL-LATEEF
The Gentle

اللَّطِيفُ

Allah is Al-Lateef, the Gentle. Al-Lateef is the One who is very gentle and kind. He is the most delicate and the most beautiful One. He creates beautiful things and knows all the small details that make them special. Al-Lateef is the opposite of violence. It is the opposite of clumsy, awkward, over-bearing or loud. Al-Lateef also means to know subtle, mysterious, or hidden knowledge.

Petals are so soft and delicate to the touch. When petals fall, they move slowly and gracefully, landing gently. The petals of a flower also open up very delicately; it is a gentle process. Think about how you feel when you are in a garden filled with beautiful flowers. Flowers are calming and peaceful. This, too, reflects Allah's gentleness.

Have you ever dropped a feather from a height and watched it fall to the ground? Just like petals, feathers are soft and gentle. They move slowly and gracefully, swaying and drifting gently through the air. When the feather finally reaches the ground, it does so with almost no impact, landing softly. This simple act of a feather falling to the ground is an amazing illustration of Al-Lateef. Next time you find a bird's feather, drop it from a height and watch it fall. Remind yourself that Allah is Al-Lateef, the Gentle.

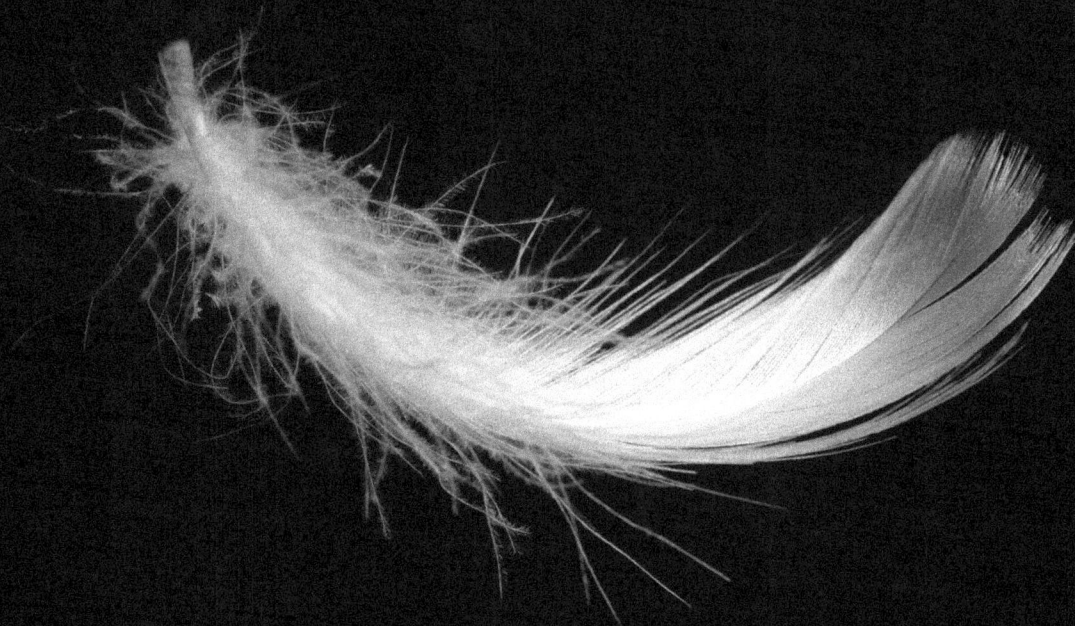

www.ingramcontent.com/pod-product-compliance
Lightning Source LLC
Chambersburg PA
CBHW060800150426

42813CB00058B/2780